I0455623

ST 31-205

US ARMY
SPECIAL FORCES
CACHING
TECHNIQUES

US ARMY
JOHN F. KENNEDY
SPECIAL WARFARE CENTER

DECEMBER 1982

The purpose of this special text (ST) is to describe the techniques and to give guidance for Special Forces (SF) caching operations. Material in this text is structured to meet the requirements of students and instructors of the Special Operations Forces School.

This text is provided for resident and nonresident instruction at the US Army Institute for Military Assistance (USAIMA). It reflects the current thought of USAIMA and conforms to Department of the Army doctrine as closely as possible.

Users of this text are encouraged to submit recommended changes or comments for improvement. Recommendations should be keyed to specific page, paragraph, and line of text. All recommendations should be addressed to:

Commandant
US Army Institute for Military Assistance
ATTN: ATSU-SF-TO
Fort Bragg, North Carolina 28307

The use of the words "he," "his," "himself, " etc. , in this special text is intended to include both the masculine and feminine genders. Any exception to this will be so noted.

i

CONTENTS

CHAPTER 1. CACHING CONSIDERATIONS   1-1

            1-1. DEFINITION   1-1

            1-2. OPERATIONAL USES   1-1

            1-3. STEPS IN CACHING   1-1
                  Selection of the Material   1-1
                  Procurement   1-1
                  Selection of Site   1-1
                      Initial Considerations   1-1
                      Relative Evaluation of Caching Methods   1-3

            1-4. CRITERIA FOR THE SITE   1-4
                  Accessibility   1-4
                  The Alternate Site   1-5
                  The Concealment Site   1-5
                  The Burial Site   1-6
                  The Submersion Site   1-7

            1-5. FINDING THE SITE   1-8
                  The Map Survey   1-8
                  The Personal Reconnaissance   1-8
                  Reference Points for Locating a Site   1-8
                  Pinpointing Techniques   1-9
                  Measuring Distances   1-13
                  Marking the Point of Emplacement   1-13
                  Additional Data Required for Emplacement   1-13

CHAPTER 2. PACKAGING   2-1

            2-1. GENERAL   2-1

            2-2. DETERMINING FACTORS   2-1

            2-3. STEPS IN THE PACKAGING OPERATION   2-2
                  Inspection   2-2
                  Cleaning   2-2
                  Drying   2-2
                  Coating with a Preservative   2-2
                  Wrapping   2-2
                  Packing   2-2
                  Instructions for Use of Cached Equipment   2-3
                  Sealing   2-3

CHAPTER 1

CACHING CONSIDERATIONS

1-1. DEFINITION

Caching is the process of hiding equipment or materials in a secure storage place with the view to future recovery for operational use.

1-2. OPERATIONAL USES

Caches have utility in a variety of operational situations, but three types of situations are particularly noteworthy.

a. First, cached supplies can meet emergency needs where personnel may be barred from their normal supply sources by sudden developments, or travel documents and extra funds may be needed for quick escape.

b. Second, caching can help solve the supply problems of long-term operations conducted far from a secure base.

c. A third use of caching is to provide for anticipated needs of wartime operations in areas likely to be overrun by the enemy.

1-3. STEPS IN CACHING

Caching is a complex operation. From start to finish it involves the following steps: selection of material, procurement of material, and selection of the site.

a. Selection of the Material. Selection of the material to be cached requires a precise estimate of what will be needed by particular units and particular operations.

b. Procurement. Procurement of the material usually represents no special problems. In fact, the relative ease of procurement before an emergency arises is one of the prime considerations in favor of caching.

c. Selection of Site. Selection of the site entails careful consideration of two factors:

(1) Initial considerations.

(a) Contents and purpose of the cache. Planning for a caching operation must start with the purpose and contents of each cache because these basic factors influence the location of the cache as well as the method of hiding. For instance, small barter items can be cached at any secure site that is accessible to the intended user, since, once recovered, they can be concealed rather easily on the person. However, since it would be very difficult to conceal rifles for a guerrilla band after removal from a cache, the site must be in an isolated area where the band can establish at least temporary control. Sometimes it is impossible to locate a cache where it would be most convenient for the intended user. All logistical objectives should be considered, however, and a sensible compromise made between objectives and actual possibilities with security always the overriding consideration.

(b) Anticipated enemy action. In planning caching operations, planners must consider the current capabilities of any intelligence or security services not participating in the operation and also the potential hazards presented by their witting and unwitting accomplices. If the caching is undertaken for wartime operational purposes, ultimate success will depend largely on whether the planners anticipate the various obstacles to recovery which the enemy and his accomplices will create if the enemy occupies the area. What are the possibilities that the enemy will preempt an apparently ideal site for one reason or another and thus deny access to it? A vacant field surrounded by brush may seem ideal for a particular cache because it is near several highways. But will the strategic location invite the enemy to locate an ordnance depot where the cache would be buried?

(c) Activities of the local population. Probably more dangerous than deliberate enemy action are all of the chance circumstances that may result in the discovery of the cache. Normal activity, such as a new building, may uncover it or impede access to it. Bad luck cannot be anticipated, but probably the best hope of avoiding it lies in careful and imaginative observation of the locality and of the people who reside in the vicinity of a prospective cache site. If the cache is intended for wartime use, the planner must attempt to imagine how the local residents will react to the pressures of war and conquest. To mention only one of the more likely reactions, a Communist regime probably will confiscate personal funds and valuables, and many local residents may resort to caching as a means of avoiding confiscation. If caching becomes popular, any likely cache site will receive much more attention than it normally does.

(d) Intended actions by Allied forces. Since the use of one site for several covert operations involves a risk of mutual compromise, some otherwise suitable caching sites should be ruled out because they have been selected for other clandestine purposes, such as drops or safehouses. Also, a site should not be located where it may be destroyed or rendered inaccessible by bombing or other Allied military action, should the area be occupied by the enemy. Moreover, installations likely to be objects of special protective efforts by the occupying enemy are certain to be inaccessible to the ordinary citizen. Therefore, if the cache is intended for wartime use, one should avoid areas such as those near key bridges, railroad intersections, power plants, and munitions factories.

(e) Packaging and transportation assets. After assessing all of the potential obstacles and hazards that a prospective cache site would present, the planner should consider whether the operational assets of the organization are sufficient to overcome all obstacles securely. It is especially necessary to consider the assets that could be used for packaging and transporting the package to the site. Best results are obtained when the packaging is done by experts at a packaging center. The first question, therefore, is to decide whether the package can be transported from the headquarters or the field packaging center to the cache site securely and soon enough to meet the operational schedules. If not, the packaging must be done locally, perhaps in a safehouse located within a few miles of the cache site. If such an arrangement is necessary, the choice of the cache sites may be restricted by limited safehouse possibilities.

(f) Personnel assets. Since anyone who participates directly in the emplacement operation knows where the cache is located, it is of utmost importance that only the most reliable persons be chosen to participate, and that no more than the necessary number be employed. The planner must consider how far the persons being used will be from their regular residence to a prospective cache site and what action cover will be required for their trip. Sometimes the transportation and cover difficulties require that the site be within a limited distance of the person's residence. The above considerations also apply to the recovery personnel.

(2) Relative evaluation of caching methods. Choice of the caching method to be used depends on the particular situation. It is therefore unsound to lay down any general rules, with one exception. Always think in terms of suitability: the method most suitable for each cache, considering its specific purpose, the actual situation in the particular locality, and the changes that may occur if the enemy gains control.

(a) Concealment. This method requires the employment of permanent man-made or natural features of the area to hide or disguise the presence of the cache. It has several advantages. Both emplacement and recovery usually can be accomplished with minimum time and labor, and a cache concealed inside a building or dry cave is protected from the elements, consequently requiring less elaborate packaging. Also, in some cases, a concealed cache can be readily inspected from time to time to insure that it is still usable. However, there is always present the unpredictable chance of accidental discovery in addition to all the hazards of wartime that may result in discovery or destruction of a concealed cache or denial of access to the site. The concealment method, therefore, is most suitable in cases where an exceptionally secure site is available or where a need for quick access to the cache justifies a calculated sacrifice in security. Concealment may range from the securing of small gold coins under a tile in the floor to walling up artillery in caves.

(b) Burial. In contrast to concealment, burial in the ground is a laborious and time-consuming method of caching, but once in place, a properly buried cache is generally secure. The difficulties encountered in burial are threefold:

1. First, burial almost always requires a high-quality container or special wrapping to protect the cache from moisture, chemicals, and bacteria in the soil.

2. Second, emplacement or recovery of a buried cache usually takes so long that the operation must be done after dark unless the site is exceptionally secluded.

<u>3</u>. <u>Third</u>, it is especially difficult to identify and locate a buried cache.

Against all these drawbacks, however, stands the hard fact that in most cases, burial is the best way of achieving lasting security. Sites suitable for secure concealment or submersion caches are few and far between, but adequate burial sites can be found almost anywhere.

(c) Submersion. The container of a submerged cache must meet such high technical standards for waterproofing and resistance to external pressure that the use of field expedients is seldom workable. To insure that a submerged cache will remain dry and in place, the planner is faced with ascertaining not only the depth of the water, but the type of bottom, the currents, and other facts that are relatively difficult for nonspecialists to obtain covertly. The emplacement operation likewise requires a high degree of skill, and at least two agents are usually essential for both emplacement and recovery. Especially when a heavy package is involved, recovery is frequently more difficult than emplacement and requires additional equipment. In view of the complications--especially the difficulty of recovery--the submersion method has been found suitable only on rare occasions. The most noteworthy usage is the relatively rare maritime resupply operation where it is impossible to deliver supplies directly to a reception committee. Caching supplies offshore by submersion is often preferable to sending a landing party ashore to make a buried cache.

1-4. CRITERIA FOR THE SITE

a. <u>Accessibility</u>. When selecting a cache site, one should always keep in mind that the site must be accessible not only for emplacement, but also for recovery of the material whenever it may be needed. Even though the most careful estimates of future operational conditions cannot insure that a cache will be accessible when it is needed, there are three questions that can and should be definitely answered before emplacement.

(1) <u>First</u>, can the site be located by simple instructions, unmistakably clear to someone who has never visited the location? A site may be ideal in every other respect, but it must be ruled out if there are no distinct, permanent landmarks within a readily measurable distance.

(2) <u>Second</u>, are there at least two secure routes to the site? An alternate escape route offers hope of avoiding detection and capture in an emergency. Both routes should provide natural concealment so that the emplacement party and the recovery party can visit the site without being seen by any person normally in the vicinity.

(3) <u>Third</u>, can the cache be emplaced and recovered at the chosen site in all seasons of the year? Snow and frozen ground make special problems for a buried cache. Whatever method is used, snow on the ground is a hazard because it is impossible to obliterate a trail in the snow. Also, one must consider whether seasonal changes in the foliage will leave the site and the routes dangerously exposed.

b. The Alternate Site. As a general rule it is advisable to select an alternate site in case unforeseen difficulties should prevent use of the best site. Unless the primary site is in a completely deserted area, there is always some danger that the emplacement party will find it occupied as they approach, or that the party will be observed as they near the site. The alternate site should be far enough away to be screened from view from the primary site, but near enough so that the party can reach it without making a second trip. The distance between the two sites will depend upon the terrain.

c. The Concealment Site.

(1) The sites for concealed caches are similar to drop sites. For purposes of caching as it is here defined, however, there are three principal differences. First, a concealment site must be far more durable than a drop. Second, the time factor in the accessibility requirements for a cache site usually is less pressing. Use of a drop often requires precise timing to conform to a tight operational schedule; unless a cache is intended for escape purposes, immediate access at a precise time is seldom necessary. Third, greater capacity is usually required of a cache site, since a drop is seldom used for equipment.

(2) A site that looks ideal for concealment may reveal itself to the opposition for that very reason. A promising site may be equally attractive to a native of an occupied country as the place to hide his valuables. The only real key to the ideal concealment site is inspired, meticulous casing, combined with great familiarity with local residents and their customs. The following list of likely concealment sites is intended merely to illustrate the possibilities:

(a) natural caves and caverns, abandoned mines and quarries,

(b) walls (behind loose bricks or stones or hidden behind the plastered surface),

(c) abandoned buildings,

(d) infrequently used structures (stadiums and other recreational facilities, railroad facilities on spur lines),

(e) memorial edifices (mausoleums, crypts, monuments),

(f) public buildings (museums, churches, libraries),

(g) ruins of historical interest,

(h) culverts,

(i) sewers, and

(j) cable conduits.

(3) Some of the criteria for a concealment site are:

(a) The site must be equally accessible to the emplacer and the recovery individual. Visits to certain interior sites may be incompatible with the cover of the emplacer or the recovery individual. For instance, a site in a house owned by a relative of the emplacer may be unsuitable because there is no adequate pretext for the recovery individual to enter the building if he has no personal connection with the owner.

(b) The site must remain accessible as long as the cache may be needed. If access to a building depends upon an individual's personal relationship with the owner, the death of the owner or the sale of the property might render it inaccessible.

(c) Discovery of a cache on the site must not compromise any person involved in the operation. Even if a cache is completely sterile, as every cache should be, the mere fact that it has been placed in a particular site may compromise certain persons. To continue the foregoing example, if the cache were discovered by the police, they could be led to suspect the emplacer because it was found in his relative's house.

(d) The site must not be frequented by potentially hostile persons. A site in a museum, for instance, would be insecure if police guards or curious visitors frequently entered the room.

(e) The site must be physically secure for the preservation of the cached material. Most buildings involve a risk that the cache may be destroyed or damaged by fire, especially in wartime. The risk may be slight, but it should be considered and weighed against the advantages of an interior site.

(4) A custodian may serve to facilitate access to a building or to guard a cache. Use of such an individual is considered inadvisable, however, as a custodian poses an additional security risk. He may use the contents of the cache for personal profit or reveal its location for other reasons.

d. The Burial Site. In the selection of a burial site, the following special factors should be considered along with the basic considerations of suitability and accessibility:

(1) Drainage. This includes the elevation of the site and the type of soil. The importance of good drainage makes a site on high ground preferable unless other considerations rule it out. Moisture is one of the greatest natural threats to the contents of the cache, and swamp muck is the most difficult soil to work in. If the site is near a stream or river, it is especially important to ascertain that the cache is well above the all-year high-water mark so that it will not be uncovered if the soil is washed away during the flood season.

(2) Ground cover. The types of vegetation at the site will influence the choice. Roots of deciduous trees make digging very difficult; coniferous trees have less extensive root systems. Also, the presence of coniferous trees usually means that the site is well drained. Does the vegetation show paths or other indications that the site is frequented too much for secure

caching? Can the ground cover be easily restored to normal appearance when burial is completed? Tall grass reveals that it has been trampled, while an overlay of leaves and humus can be replaced easily and will effectively conceal a freshly refilled hole.

(3) Natural concealment. The vegetation or the surrounding terrain should offer natural concealment for the burial and recovery parties working at the site. Seasonal variations in the foliage should be considered carefully.

(4) Type of soil. Sandy loam is ideal because it is easy to dig and drains well. Clay soil should be avoided because it becomes quite sticky in wet weather and during a dry season it may become so hard that it is almost impossible to dig.

(5) Snowfall and freezing. Data on the normal snowfall, the depth to which the ground freezes in winter, and the usual dates of freezing and thawing influence the choice of the site if there is any possibility that the cache must be buried or recovered in winter. Frozen ground impedes digging and at best requires special consideration in computing the time allotted for burial or recovery. Snow on the ground is especially hazardous for the burial operation. It is practically impossible to restore the snow over the excavation to normal appearance unless one is favored with more snowfall or a brisk wind at the propitious moment. Furthermore, it is very difficult to make sure that no traces of the operation will be left after the snow has melted.

(6) Rocks and other subsurface obstructions. The presence of any large obstructions that might make it impossible to use a particular site can be determined to some extent before digging by probing with a rod or stake at the exact spot selected for the cache.

e. The Submersion Site.

(1) To be suitable for a submerged cache, a body of water must have certain characteristics that can be determined only by a thorough survey of the site. The importance of these characteristics will be understood after familiarization with the technicalities of submersion (discussed in the section on emplacement). Meanwhile, it should be noted that submersion usually requires a boat, first for reconnoitering, then for emplacement. Thus the special accessibility problems involved in submersion usually narrow down to availability of a boat and action cover for using it. If there is no fishing or pleasure boating at the site, the cover for this peculiar type boating may be a real problem.

(2) In tropical areas the course of streams or rivers is frequently changed by the seasonal rainfall and can cause many problems. This fact should be kept in mind in relation both to the choice of sites and to the selection of reference points.

1-5. FINDING THE SITE

a. <u>The Map Survey</u>. Finding the site that meets the criteria described above is frequently difficult and usually requires a thorough systematic survey of the general area designated for the cache. The first phase of the survey is best done with as large scale a map of the area as is available. By close scrutiny of the map the planner can soon determine whether a particular sector must be ruled out as being too near factories, homes, busy thoroughfares, or probable military targets in wartime. A good military-type map will also suggest the positive features in the topography: proximity to adequate roads or trails, natural concealment in the form of surrounding woods or groves, and adequate drainage. A map also will show the natural and man-made features in the landscape. It will provide the indispensable reference points for locating a cache site: confluences of streams, dams and waterfalls, road junctures and distance markers, villages, bridges, churches, and cemeteries.

b. <u>The Personal Reconnaissance</u>.

(1) A map survey normally should yield the location of several promising sites within the general area designated for the cache. In order to select and pinpoint the best site, however, it is essential for a well-qualified observer to examine each site first hand. If possible, whoever examines the site should be provided with adequate maps, a compass, a drawing pad or board for making sketch maps or tracings, and a metallic measuring line. (A wire knotted at regular intervals is adequate for measuring. Twine or cloth measuring tapes should not be used because stretching or shrinkage will make them inaccurate if they get wet.) A probe rod also should be provided for probing prospective burial sites, if it can be carried securely.

(2) Since the observer can seldom hope to complete his field survey without being noticed by local residents, his action cover is of utmost importance. The cover must fit the individual as well as offer a natural explanation for his exploratory activity in the area. Ordinarily this means that either the observer poses as a tourist or other newcomer with some pretext for visiting the locality, or else his action cover must be developed over an extended period before he undertakes actual reconnaissance. For instance, a known resident of the locality cannot suddenly take up hunting, fishing, or wildlife photography without arousing interest and perhaps suspicion; he must build up a reputation for being a devotee of his sport or hobby.

c. <u>Reference Points for Locating a Site</u>.

(1) When a suitable cache site has been found, the final and absolutely essential requirement is that it can be located readily by simple, unmistakable instructions. The instructions must identify the <u>general area</u> (the generally recognizable place names, from the country down to the nearest village) and an <u>immediate reference point</u> (IRP), which can be any durable landmark definitely identifiable by title or simple description (the only Roman Catholic Church in a certain village, the only bridge on a named road between two villages). The instructions must also include a <u>final reference</u>

point (FRP), which must meet four requirements.

(a) First, it must be definitely identifiable, including at least one feature that can be used as a precise reference point.

(b) Second, it must be an object that will remain fixed as long as the cache may be used.

(c) Third, it must be near enough to the cache to pinpoint the exact location of the cache by precise linear measurements from the FRP to the cache.

(d) Fourth, the FRP should be related to the IRP by a simple route description, proceeding from the IRP to the FRP.

(2) Since the route description should be reduced to the minimum essential, the ideal solution for locating the cache is to combine the IRP and the FRP in one landmark readily identifiable but sufficiently secluded to permit locating the cache nearby. These criteria may be met sometimes by the following objects: small, unfrequented bridges and dams, boundary markers, kilometer markers and culverts along unfrequented roads, geodetic survey markers, battle monuments, and wayside shrines. When such ideal reference points are not available at an otherwise suitable site, natural or man-made objects such as the following may serve as FRP: large rocks, posts for power or telephone lines, intersections in stone fences or hedgerows, and gravestones in isolated cemeteries.

d. Pinpointing Techniques. It is absolutely essential that the recovery instructions identify the exact location of the cache. This is done by describing the point where it is placed in terms that relate it to the FRP. When the concealment method is used, the cache ordinarily is placed inside the FRP so it is pinpointed by a precise description of the FRP. A submerged cache usually is pinpointed by describing exactly how the moorings are attached to the FRP. With a buried cache, any of the following techniques may be used:

(1) Placing directly beside the FRP. The simplest method is to place the cache directly beside the FRP. Then the pinpointing problem is reduced to specifying a precise reference point on the FRP. (See Sketch 1.)

(2) Sighting by projection. This method can be used if the FRP has one flat side long enough to permit precise sighting by projecting a line along the side of the object. The cache is placed a measured distance along the sighted line. (See Sketch 2.) This method can also be used if two precise FRPs are available, by projecting a line sighted between the two objects. In either case, the instructions for finding the cache must state the approximate direction of the cache from the FRP. Since small errors in sighting are magnified as the sighted line is extended, the cache should be placed as close to the FRP as other factors permit. Ordinarily this method becomes unreliable if the sighted line is extended beyond 50 meters.

Sketch 1. Cache is located adjacent to S.W. corner of church on S. side.

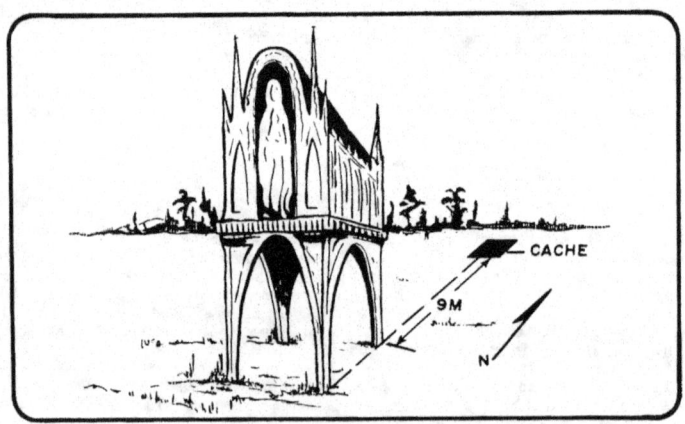

Sketch 2. Cache is located 9 meters N. of N.E. corner in line with N.E. side of shrine.

(3) Placing at the intersection of measured lines. If two FRPs are available within several paces, the cache can be one line being projected from each of the FRPs. (See Sketch 3.) If this method is used, the approximate direction of the cache from each FRP must be stated. To insure accuracy, neither of the projected lines (from the FRPs to the point of emplacement) should be more than twice as long as the base line (between the two FRPs). If this proportion is maintained, the only limitation upon the length of the projected lines is the length of the measuring line that the recovery party is expected to carry. <u>Two</u> measuring lines should be provided when this method is used.

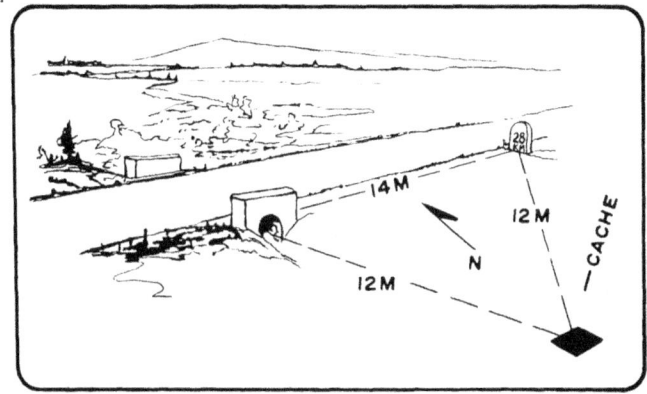

Sketch 3. Cache is located 12 meters S.W. of kilometer stone 28 and 12 meters S.E. from center of S. end of culvert 14 meters W. of kilometer stone 28.

(4) Sighting by compass azimuth.

(a) If the above methods of sighting are not feasible, one measured line may be projected by taking a compass azimuth from the FRP to the point where the cache is placed. (See Sketch 4.) To avoid confusion, it is preferable to use an azimuth to a cardinal point of the compass (north, east, south, or west). Since compass sightings are likely to be inaccurate, a cache that is pinpointed by this method should not be placed more than ten meters from the FRP.

(b) Sketch 5 illustrates how sighting by compass azimuth can be combined with placing at the intersection of measured lines when only one FRP is available but a multiple cache is required. (A multiple cache is usually employed for communications equipment.) Whenever possible, it is preferable to use several FRPs for pinpointing a multiple cache, as illustrated by Sketch 13 (see appendix A).

1-11

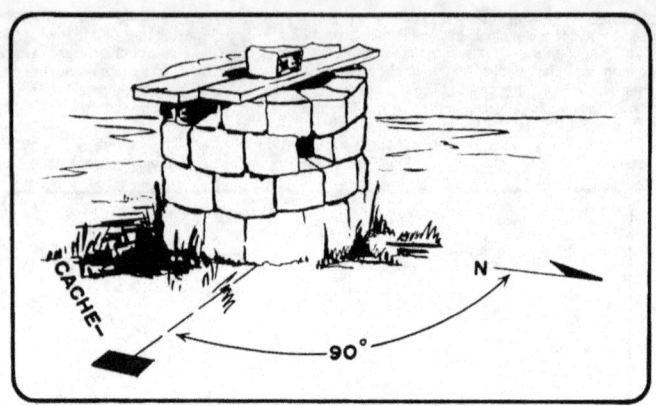

Sketch 4. Cache is located 3 meters from center of well
on compass reading of 90º.

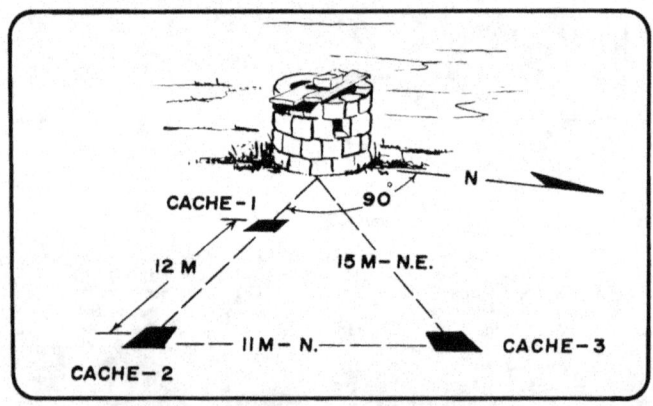

Sketch 5. Cache 1 is located 3 meters from center of well on compass bearing
of 90º. Cache 2 is 12 meters from cache 1 on extension of line
between cache 1 and center of well. Cache 3 is 15 meters N.E.
center of well and 11 meters N. of cache 2.

d. Measuring Distances.

(1) All measured distances should be expressed in a linear system the recovery agent is sure to understand—ordinarily the standard system for the country where the cache is located. Whole numbers (6 meters, not 6.3 or 6 1/2) should be used in order to keep recovery instructions as brief as possible. It should be stressed one cannot obtain whole numbers by selecting the exact location for the cache, then taking sightings and measurements. Ordinarily one should start with the idea of keeping all measurements as simple as possible and proceed to locate the cache accordingly.

(2) If the surface of the ground between the points to be measured is uneven, the linear distance should be measured on a direct line from point to point, rather than by following the contour of the ground. This procedure requires a measuring line long enough to reach the full distance from point to point and strong enough to be pulled taut without risk of breaking.

e. Marking the Point of Emplacement.

(1) The emplacement operation can be simplified and critical time saved if the point where the cache is to be buried is marked during the reconnaissance.

(2) If a night burial is planned, it may be necessary to mark the point of emplacement during a daylight reconnaissance, and this procedure should be used whenever operational conditions permit.

(3) The marker must be an object that is meaningless to an unwitting observer, but easily recognized—such as a small rock or a branch with the butt placed at the point selected for the emplacement.

f. Additional Data Required for Emplacement.

(1) During his personal reconnaissance the observer must not only pinpoint the cache site, but also gather all the incidental information required for planning the emplacement operation. It is especially important to determine the best route to the site and at least one alternate route, the security hazards along these routes, and any information that can be used to overcome the hazards.

(2) Since these data will also be essential for the recovery operation, they must be included in the final cache report compiled after emplacement. Therefore, the observer should be thoroughly familiar with the "Twelve-Point Cache Report" (appendix A) before he starts his reconnaissance. This report is used as a checklist and he should attempt to observe and record as much as possible of the data specified in this checklist, particularly points 6 through 9 and 11. The initial reconnaissance also provides an excellent opportunity for a preliminary estimate of the time required for getting to the site from some arbitrary starting point.

CHAPTER 2

PACKAGING

2-1. GENERAL

Packaging usually involves not only packing the material to be cached, but
also additional processing in order to protect the material from all the
adverse storage conditions encountered in caching. The importance of proper
packaging can scarcely be exaggerated when it is remembered that inadequate
packaging very likely will result in the material's being unusable when it is
needed. Since special equipment and skilled technicians are needed for best
results, it is advisable that packaging be done at headquarters or a field
packaging center whenever possible. Accordingly, the following discussion is
intended primarily to familiarize operational personnel with the fundamentals
of the subject, so that they can improvise field expedients for emergency use.

2-2. DETERMINING FACTORS

    a. The first rule of packaging is that all processing will be tailored to
fit the specific requirements of each cache.

    b. The method of packaging, as well as the size, shape, and weight of the
package will be determined by the material to be cached, the caching method to
be employed, and especially how the cached material will be recovered and
used. For instance, if it is anticipated that circumstances may require one
man to recover the cache by himself, the container should be no larger than a
small suitcase, and the total weight of container and contents no more than 30
pounds. Of course these limits must be exceeded with some equipment, but the
need for larger packages should be weighed against the difficulties and risks
in handling them. Even if more than one person is available for recovery, the
material should be divided whenever possible into separate packages of a size
and weight readily portable by one man.

    c. Another very important consideration in packaging concerns adverse
storage conditions. Any or all of the following conditions may be present:
moisture, external pressure, freezing temperatures, and the bacteria and
corrosive chemicals found in some soil and water. Animal life may present a
hazard; insects and rodents may attack the package. If the cache is concealed
in an exterior site, larger animals also may threaten it. Whether the
packaging is adequate usually will depend upon how carefully the conditions at
the site have been analyzed and considered in designing the cache. Thus, the
method of caching (burial, concealment, or submersion) should be determined
before the packaging is done.

    d. It is equally important to consider how long the cache is intended to
be usable. Since one can seldom be sure when the cache will be needed, it is
a sound rule to design the packaging to withstand adverse storage conditions
for at least as long as the normal shelf life of the equipment in the cache.

2-3. STEPS IN THE PACKAGING OPERATION

The exact procedure for packaging will depend upon the specific requirements for the cache and upon what packaging equipment is available. The following description includes the steps that are almost always necessary.

a. Inspection. The equipment to be cached is inspected immediately before packaging in order to make sure it is complete, in serviceable condition, and free of all corrosive or contaminative substances.

b. Cleaning. It is especially important that all corrodible items be cleaned thoroughly immediately before the final preservative coating is applied. All foreign matter, including any preservative applied before the article was shipped to the field, should be removed completely. Throughout the packaging operation, all contents of the cache should be handled with rubber or freshly cleaned cotton gloves, because even minute particles of human sweat will corrode metallic equipment, and also because fingerprints on any material in the cache might enable the opposition to identify those who did the packaging.

c. Drying. When cleaning is completed, every trace of moisture must be removed from all corrodible items. Several methods of drying may be used: wiping with a highly absorbent cloth, heating, or application of a desiccant. Usually heating is best, unless the material can be damaged by heat. To dry by heating, the equipment to be cached should be placed in an oven for at least three hours at a temperature of about 110°F. An oven can be improvised from a large metal can or drum. Especially in a humid climate, it is important to dry the oven thoroughly before using it by heating to at least 212°F. Then the equipment should be inserted as soon as the oven cools down to about 110°F. If a desiccant is used, it should not be allowed to touch any metallic surface. Silica gel is a satisfactory desiccant, and it is commonly available.

d. Coating With a Preservative. A light coating of oil is applied to weapons, tools, and other articles with unpainted metallic surfaces. A coat of paint may suffice for other metal objects.

e. Wrapping. When drying and coating are completed, the items to be cached are wrapped in a suitable material (see para 2-4 below) that should be as nearly waterproof as possible. Each article should be wrapped separately, so that one perforation in the wrapping will not expose all items in the cache. The wrapping should fit tightly to each object in order to eliminate air pockets, and all folds should be sealed with a waterproof substance.

f. Packing. Several simple rules must be observed when packing equipment in the container.

(1) All moisture must be removed from the interior of the container by heating or application of a desiccant, and a long-lasting desiccant should be packed inside the container to absorb any residual moisture. If silica gel is used, the required amount can be calculated by using the ratio of 15 kilograms of silica gel to one cubic meter of storage space within the container. (This figure is based on two assumptions: the container is completely moistureproof, and the contents are slightly moist when inserted.)

2-2

Therefore, the ratio allows an ample margin for incomplete drying and can be reduced if the drying process is known to be highly effective.

(2) Air pockets should be eliminated as far as possible by tight packing. Padding which has been thoroughly dried should be used liberally to fill air pockets and also to protect the contents from shock. Clothing and other materials, which will also be useful to the recovery agents, should be used for padding if possible. Objects made of different metals should never be allowed to touch, since continued contact may cause corrosion through electrolytic action.

g. Instructions For Use of Cached Equipment. Written instructions and diagrams should be included if they will facilitate assembly or use of the cached equipment. Instructions must be written in a language the agent can understand, and the wording should be as simple as possible and unmistakably clear. Diagrams should be self-explanatory since the eventual user may not be able to read an explanatory text despite best efforts to anticipate language difficulties.

h. Sealing. When packing is completed, the lid of the container is sealed to make it watertight. Whatever sealing device is used, utmost care should be taken to make sure that the sealing is done properly, because the closing joint is the most vulnerable.

i. The Submersion Test. After the container is sealed, it should be tested to make sure that it is watertight by entirely submerging the container in water and watching for air bubbles escaping. Hot water should be used if possible, since hot water will bring out leaks that would not be revealed by a cold water test.

2-4. WRAPPING MATERIALS

The most important requirement for wrapping material is that it be moistureproof. Also, it should be sealed (self-sealing or adhesive to a sealing material); it should be pliable enough to fit closely, with tight folds; and it should be tough enough to resist tearing and puncturing. Pliability and toughness may be combined by using two wrappings: an inner one that is thin and pliable and an outer one of heavier material. A tough outer wrapping is essential unless the container and the padding are adequate to prevent any scraping between objects in the cache. The following materials are recommended as field expedients because they often can be obtained locally and used effectively by unskilled personnel:

a. Aluminum Foil. For use as an inner wrapping, aluminum foil is the best of the widely available materials. It is moistureproof as long as it does not become perforated, and provided the folds are adequately sealed. The drawbacks to its use for caching are that the thin foils perforate easily, while the heavy ones (over two mils thick) tend to admit moisture through the folds. The heavy-duty grade of aluminum foil generally sold for kitchen use is adequate when used with an outer wrapping. Scrim-backed foil, which is heat-sealable, is widely used commercially to package articles for shipment or storage. Portable heat-sealers which are easy to use are available commercially, or the sealing can be done with a standard household iron.

b. Moisture-resistant Papers. Several brands of commercial wrapping papers are resistant to water and grease. They do not provide lasting protection against moisture when used alone, but they are effective as an inner wrapping, to prevent rubber, wax, and similar substances from sticking to the articles in the cache.

c. Rubber Repair Gum. This is a self-sealing compound generally used for repairing tires; it makes an excellent outer wrapping. Standard commercial brands come in several thicknesses; 2 millimeters is the most satisfactory for caching. A watertight seal is produced easily by placing two rubber surfaces together and applying pressure manually. The seal should be at least a half inch wide. Since this material has a tendency to adhere to some objects, an inner wrapping of nonadhesive material must be used with it, and the backing should be left on the rubber material to keep it from sticking to other objects in the cache.

d. Grade "C" Barrier Material. This is a cloth impregnated with microcrystalline wax used extensively when packing for storage or overseas shipment. Thus it is generally available, and it has the additional advantage of being self-sealing. Although it is not as effective as rubber repair gum, it may be used as an outer wrapping over aluminum foil to prevent perforation of the foil. Used without an inner wrapping, three layers of grade "C" barrier material may keep the contents dry for as long as three months, but it is highly vulnerable to insects and rodents. Also, the wax wrapping has a low melting point and will adhere to most objects, so it should not be used without an inner wrapping except in emergencies.

e. Wax. If no wrapping material is available, an outer coating of microcrystalline wax, parrafin, or similar waxy substance can be used to protect the contents against moisture, although it will not provide protection against insects and rodents. The package should be hot-dipped in the waxy substance, or the wax can be heated to molten form and applied with a brush.

2-5. CRITERIA FOR THE CONTAINER

a. General. The outer container serves to protect the contents from shock, moisture, and the other natural hazards to which the cache may be exposed. The ideal container would have all the following qualifications:

(1) Completely watertight and airtight after sealing.

(2) Noiseless when being handled--the handles should not rattle against the body of the container.

(3) Resistant to shock and abrasion.

(4) Able to withstand crushing pressures.

(5) Lightweight construction.

(6) Able to withstand rodents, insects, and bacteria.

(7) Equipped with a sealing device that can be closed and reopened easily and repeatedly.

(8) Capable of withstanding highly acid or alkaline soil or water.

b. The Standard Stainless Steel Container.

(1) Stainless steel containers, designed particularly for burial caching, are available. These containers come in several sizes as follows:

(a) 8 1/2" X 7" X 9"

(b) 16 1/2" X 7" X 9"

(c) 40" X 7" X 9"

(d) 45" X 7" X 9"

(e) 50" X 7" X 9"

(2) Since the stainless steel container is more satisfactory than any that could be improvised in the field, it should be used whenever possible. The ideal procedure is to have the stainless steel container packed at headquarters or at a field packaging center. If the materials to be cached must be obtained locally, use of the stainless steel container is still advisable because its high resistance to moisture eliminates the need for an outer wrapping. A single wrapping usually should be employed even with the stainless steel container in order to protect the contents from any residual moisture that may be present in the container when it is sealed.

c. Field Expedient Containers. Obviously the ideal container cannot be improvised in the field, but some standard military and commercial containers can meet the essential requirements if they are adapted with care and resourcefulness. First, a container must be sufficiently sturdy to remain unpunctured and in shape through whatever rough handling or crushing pressure it may encounter. (Even a slight warping may make the joint around the lid leak.) The second critical feature of any container is the device for sealing the joint around the lid. If the lid is not already watertight and airtight, it may be possible to make it so by improvising a sealing device. The most common type includes a rubber-composition gasket or lining and a sharp metal rim which is pressed against the gasket by a clamp or spring. The gasket must be tough, and the rim sharp enough to indent the gasket without cutting it. Another common sealing device is a threaded lid. Its effectiveness can be increased by applying heavy grease to the threads. (Metallic solder should not be used for sealing because it will corrode metal surfaces when exposed to moisture). Whenever any nonstainless metal container is used, it is important to apply several coats of high-quality paint to all exterior surfaces. Following are some of the more suitable military and commercial containers:

(1) Instrument containers. Aircraft and other precision instruments ordinarily are shipped in steel containers with a waterproof sealing device. The standard instrument containers range from the half-gallon to the ten-gallon sizes. If one of suitable size can be found, it will be quite satisfactory with minimum modifications. In the most common type the only weak point is the nut and bolt that tighten the locking band around the lid. These should be replaced with a stainless steel nut and bolt.

(2) Ammunition boxes. Several standard types of steel ammunition boxes that have a rubber-gasketed closing device are satisfactory for buried caches. The advantage of ammunition boxes is that several standard sizes are usually available at a military depot.

(3) Steel drums. A caching container of suitable size may be found among the several types and sizes of steel drums that are used commercially for shipping oil, grease, nails, soap, and other products. The most common types lack an adequate sealing device, so a waterproof material should be used around the lid. Full removable head drums with lock-ring closures generally give a satisfactory seal.

(4) Glass jars. Glass has the advantages of being completely waterproof and impervious to chemicals, bacteria, and insects. Although glass is highly vulnerable to shock, glass jars of a sturdy quality can withstand the crushing pressure normally encountered in caching. However, none of the available glass containers have an adequate sealing device for the joint around the lid. The standard commercial canning jar with a spring clamp and rubber washer is watertight, but the metal clamp is vulnerable to corrosion. Therefore a glass jar with spring clamp and rubber washer is an adequate expedient for short-term caching of small objects, but it should not be relied upon to resist moisture for more than a year.

(5) Paint cans. The standard can with a reusable lid requires a waterproof adhesive around the lid. It is especially important to apply several coats of paint to the exterior because the metal in a standard commercial can is not as heavy as that in a metal drum. Even when the exterior is thoroughly painted, a paint can probably will not resist moisture for more than a few months.

CHAPTER 3

EMPLACEMENT OPERATION

3-1. BURIAL PROCEDURE

Since burial is the most frequently used method of emplacement, the complete procedure for burial will be described first, followed by a discussion of features peculiar to submersion and concealment.

a. _Horizontal and Vertical Caches._ Ordinarily the hole for a buried cached is vertical, being dug straight down from the surface. (See Sketch 6.) Sometimes a horizontal cache, with the hole dug into the side of a steep hill or bank, provides a workable solution when a suitable site on level or slightly sloping ground is not available. (See Sketch 7.) A horizontal cache may provide better drainage in areas of heavy rainfall, but it is more likely to be exposed by soil erosion and also more difficult to refill and restore to normal appearance.

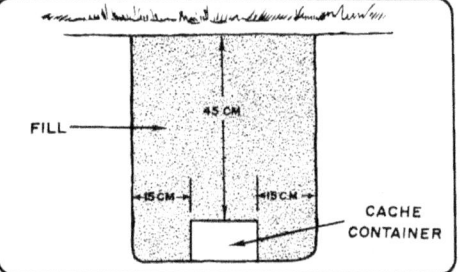

Sketch 6. Vertical hole for a buried cache.

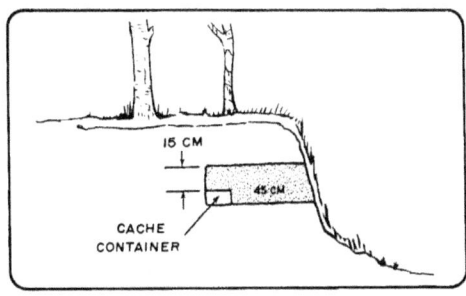

Sketch 7. Horizontal hole for a buried cache.

b. <u>Dimensions of the Hole</u>. The exact dimensions of the hole, either vertical or horizontal, depend on the size and shape of the cache container. As a general rule, to make sure that the hole will be large enough for the container to be inserted easily, the horizontal dimensions of the hole should be about 30 centimeters longer and wider than the container. Most important, it should be deep enough to permit covering the container with soil to <u>about 45 centimeters</u>. This figure is recommended for normal usage because <u>more</u> shallow burial risks exposure of the cache through soil erosion or inadvertent uncovering by normal indigenous activity. A deeper hole makes probing for recovery more difficult and unnecessarily prolongs the time required for burial and recovery.

c. <u>Shoring</u>. If there is a risk that the surrounding soil will cave in during excavation, boards or bags filled with subsoil may be used to shore the sides of the hole. Permanent shoring may be needed to protect an improvised container from pressure or shock.

d. <u>Equipment</u>. The following items of equipment may be helpful or indispensable for burying a cache, depending upon the conditions at the site:

(1) Measuring instruments—usually a wire or metal tape and compass—for pinpointing the site; paper and pencil for recording the measurements.

(2) A probe rod for locating rocks, large roots, or other obstacles in the subsoil. The probe rod should be at least as long as the depth of the hole, pointed, and equipped with a sturdy handle, so that it can be pushed into the ground by hand. A thin steel rod, approximately one centimeter in diameter, is best. The probe rod should be round, so that it can be turned (like a screwdriver) while pushing it into the ground. (Turning facilitates penetration when the ground is hard.) A handle can be improvised by making a 90-degree bend near the top of the rod. Some field expedients are: certain types of cleaning rods for rifles and machineguns; a solid curtain rod; welding rods of the proper diameter.

(3) Two ground sheets on which to place sod and loose soil. An article of clothing may be used for a small excavation if nothing else is available.

(4) Sacks (sandbags, flour sacks) for holding subsoil.

(5) A pickax, if the ground is too hard for spading.

(6) A hatchet for cutting roots.

(7) A crowbar for prying rocks.

(8) A flashlight or lamp if burial is to be done at night.

e. <u>The Burial Party</u>. When the cache has been designed and the equipment selected, every step of the emplacement operation must be carefully worked out in advance. Aside from locating, digging, and refilling the hole, the most important factors in this part of the emplacement plan may be expressed with one word: Personnel. Since it is almost impossible to prevent every member of the burial party from knowing the location of the cache, each member will be a prime security problem as long as the cache remains intact. Thus the burial party must be kept as small as possible, and each member must be selected with utmost care. Once selected, each member must have adequate cover to explain his absence from home or work during the operation, his trip to and from the site, and his possession of whatever equipment cannot be concealed on the way. Transportation for the burial party may be a problem, depending on the number of persons, how far they must go, and what equipment they must take. When all details of the operation have been worked out, every member of the burial party must be briefed on exactly what he will do from start to finish.

f. The Operational Schedule. The final step in planning the emplacement operation is to make a schedule, setting the date, time, and place for every step of the operation that requires advance coordination. The schedule will depend mainly on the circumstances, but to be practical it must include a realistic estimate of how long it will take to complete the burial. Here generalizations are worthless, and the only sure guide is actual experience under similar conditions. Speaking in the abstract, three things may be said about scheduling.

(1) First, a careful burial job probably will take longer than most novices will expect. Therefore, if circumstances require a tight schedule, it may be advisable to make a "dry run" or test exercise before taking the package to the site.

(2) Second, unless the site is exceptionally well concealed or isolated, night burial probably will be necessary to avoid detection. The difficulties of working in the dark make a nighttime practice exercise especially advisable.

(3) Third, the schedule should permit waiting for advantageous weather conditions. The difficulties of snow have already been mentioned. Rainy weather increases the problems of digging and complicates the cover story. If the burial is to be done at night, a moonless night or a heavy overcast is desirable.

g. Approaching the Site. Regardless of how effective the action cover may be for the trip to the cache site, the immediate approach must be completely unobserved to avoid detection of the burial. The point where the burial party "disappears," perhaps by turning off a road into a woods, must be carefully selected, so as to minimize the risk that the party will be observed at the critical moment. This applies likewise to the "reappearance" point, and the return trip should be by a different route. Rules for concealed movement should be strictly observed, the party proceeding cautiously and silently along a route that makes the best use of natural concealment. All this requires foresight, with special attention to natural concealment while reconnoitering the route and to the means of avoiding rattling when preparing the package and burial equipment.

h. Security Measures at the Site.

(1) Since detection of the burial party at the cache site would be disastrous, the time spent here is the most critical period in any caching operation. Therefore, it is of utmost importance to maintain maximum vigilance at the site.

(2) It is highly desirable that at least one lookout should be on guard constantly. If one man must do the burial by himself, he should pause frequently to look and listen.

(3) A flashlight or lantern should be used as little as possible, and special care should be taken to mask the glare.

(4) An emergency plan for action in case of interruption should be thought through in advance, and the burial party should be so thoroughly briefed that they will respond instantly to the danger signal.

(5) Planning should include consideration of the various escape routes and whether the party will attempt to retain the package or conceal it along the escape route.

i. Digging and Refilling. Although the exact procedure will vary slightly with the design of the cache, certain basic steps must never be overlooked. As the following description shows, the whole procedure is designed to restore the site to normal as far as possible:

(1) Mark the exact spot designated as the final pinpoint in the instructions for locating the cache.

(2) Mark the length and width of the hole, with the final pinpoint in the center.

(3) Probe the whole area designated for the hole by repeatedly inserting a probe rod in the ground, to the depth at which the bottom of the container will be placed. (Ideally, probing should be done during the preliminary reconnaissance. If it cannot be done then, thorough probing before starting to dig is highly advisable, because an obstacle discovered before digging usually can be avoided by a slight change in the location of the cache, but a large rock encountered when digging is almost completed may disrupt a tight operational schedule.)

(4) Place a ground sheet at the edge of the hole and anchor it in place.

(5) Remove the sod, taking care to cut it into rectangular pieces that can be replaced after the hole is refilled. Place the sod on the ground sheet, keeping the pieces in their original pattern.

(6) Dig the hole, keeping the topsoil separate from subsoil. Preferably this should be done by piling the topsoil on a second ground sheet and putting the subsoil in sacks. Place the filled sacks on the ground sheet,

in order to avoid leakage of subsoil onto the ground near the cache. If sacks are not available, the subsoil can be placed on a separate section of the ground sheet.

(7) Check the dimensions of the hole, making certain that the depth is exactly as planned.

(8) Place the package in the hole. If more than one package is placed on the same level, a gap of approximately three centimeters between them prevents their becoming wedged together and permits easier removal.

(9) Refill the hole, tamping the soil very firmly and frequently as it is replaced. Leave enough room at the top of the hole to replace all topsoil down to its normal depth.

(10) Replace the sod, taking special care to restore it to normal appearance.

j. Sterilizing the Site. When the hole has been refilled, a special effort should be made to insure that the site is left sterile--restored to normal in every way, with no clues left to indicate burial or the burial party's visit to the vicinity. Since sterilization is most important for the security of the operation, the schedule should allow ample time to complete these final steps in an unhurried, thorough manner:

(1) Dispose of any excess soil far enough away from the site to avoid attracting attention to the site. Flushing into a stream is the ideal solution.

(2) Check all tools and equipment against a checklist to make sure that nothing is left behind. This should include all personal items which might drop from pockets. To keep this risk to a minimum, members of the burial party should carry nothing on their persons except the essentials for doing the job and backstopping their action cover.

(3) Make a final inspection of the site for any traces of the burial. Obviously this step will be none too reliable on a dark night, so that use of a carefully prepared checklist is all the more essential. With a night burial it may be advisable to return to the site in daytime, if this can be done safely, and inspect it for telltale evidence.

3-2. SUBMERSION PROCEDURE

a. Weighting and Mooring. Emplacing a submerged cache always involves two basic steps: weighting the container to keep it from floating to the surface, and mooring to keep it in place. The moorings must also serve a second function--to provide a handle for pulling the cache to the surface when it is recovered. Ordinarily the weights rest on the bottom of the lake or river and function as anchors, and the moorings connect the anchors to the container. If these moorings are not accessible for recovery, another line must extend from the cache to a fixed, accessible object in the water or on shore. There are four types of moorings.

(1) Spider web moorings. The container is attached to several mooring cables that radiate to anchors placed around the cache, forming a web. The container must be buoyant, so that it lifts the cables far enough off the bottom to be readily secured by grappling. The site must be located exactly at time of emplacement by visual sightings to fixed landmarks in the water or along the shore, using several FRPs to establish a point where two sighted lines intersect. (See Sketch 8.) For recovery, the site is located by taking sightings on the reference points, then a mooring cable is engaged by dragging the bottom or diving. This method of mooring is most difficult for recovery. It can be used only where the bottom is smooth and firm enough for dragging, or where the water is not too deep, cold, or murky for diving.

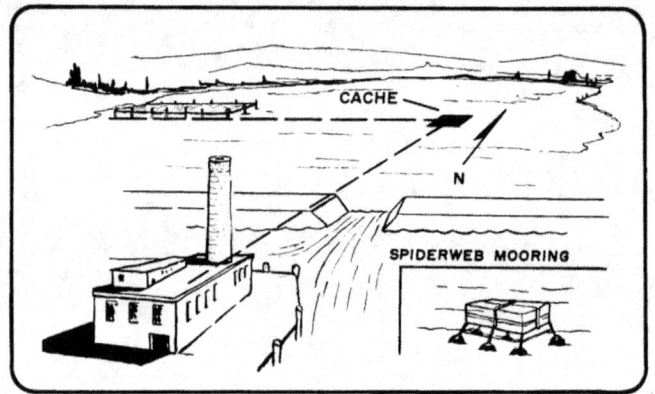

Sketch 8. Cache is located in line with south side of pier and on extension line between east side of spillway and chimney of paper mill, south of pond.

(2) Line-to-shore mooring. The container is weighted with an attached anchor, and a line is run from the cache to an immovable object along the shore. (See Sketch 9.) The section of the line that extends from the shore to this object must be buried in the ground or otherwise well concealed.

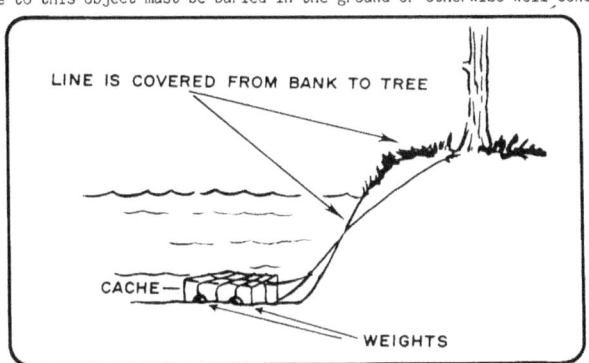

LINE IS COVERED FROM BANK TO TREE

CACHE—

WEIGHTS

Sketch 9. Line-to-shore mooring.

(3) Buoy mooring. The container is anchored, and a line is run from the cache to a buoy or other fixed, floating marker, then fastened well below the waterline. (See Sketch 10.) This method is secure only as long as the buoy is left in place. It is common practice to inspect and repaint buoys every six months or so, and the schedule should be determined before a buoy is used.

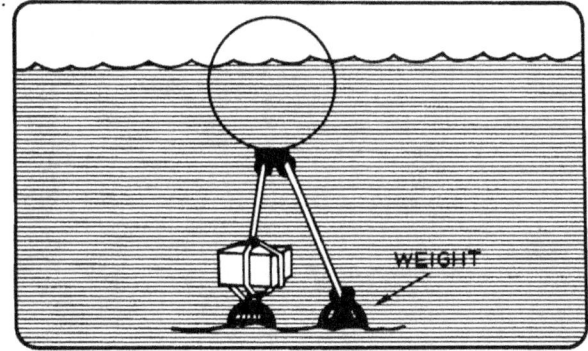

WEIGHT

Sketch 10. Buoy mooring.

(4) Structural mooring. The container is anchored, and a line for retrieving it is run to a bridge pier or other solid structure in the water. (See Sketch 11.) The line must be fastened well below the low-water mark.

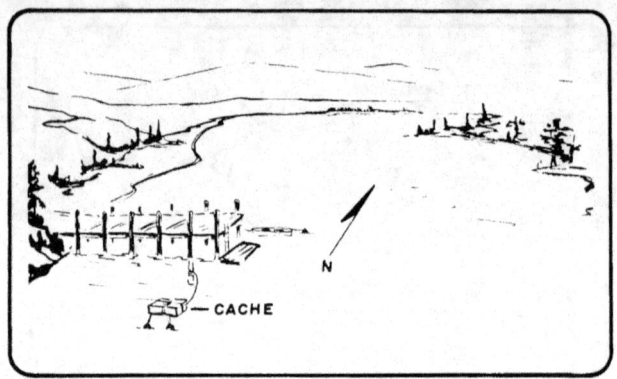

Sketch 11. Cache is moored to fifth piling from west end of pier on south side.

b. Essential Data for Submersion. Whatever type of mooring is used, it is evident that certain data must be determined beforehand and carefully considered in designing a submerged cache. The cache very likely will be lost if any of these critical factors are overlooked.

(1) Buoyancy. Many containers are buoyant even when filled, and it is most important that the container be weighted sufficiently to submerge it and keep it in place. If the contents do not provide enough weight, the balance must be made up by attaching an anchor weight to the container. The buoyancy problem may be illustrated by the following table, which applies to several sizes of the standard stainless steel container.

Container dimensions (inches)	Empty container weight (pounds)	Approximate weight that must be added to empty container weight to attain zero buoyancy (pounds)
7 x 9 x 8 1/2	5	15
7 x 9 x 16 1/2	8	31
7 x 9 x 40	16	77
7 x 9 x 45	17 1/2	88
7 x 9 x 50	19	97

The weighting required for any container can be calculated theoretically if the displacement of the container and the gross weight of container plus contents are known. This calculation may be useful for designing an anchor weight, but it never should be relied upon for actual emplacement. In order to avoid hurried improvisation during emplacement, the buoyancy always should be tested in advance by actual submersion of the container with weighting attached. This sinking test determines only that a submerged cache will not float to the surface; additional weighting is required to keep it from drifting along the bottom. As a general rule, the additional weight should be at least one tenth of the gross weight required to make the container sink; more weight is advisable if strong currents are present.

(2) Submersion depth. The depth at which the container is to be submerged must be determined in order to calculate the water pressure that the container must withstand. The greater the depth, the greater the danger that the container will be crushed by water pressure. For instance, the standard stainless steel burial container will buckle at a depth of approximately 4.3 meters. The difficulty of waterproofing likewise increases with depth. Thus the container should not be submerged any deeper than necessary to avoid detection. As a general rule, 2.2 meters is the maximum advisable depth for caching. If seasonal or tidal variations in the water level require deeper submersion, the container should be tested by actual submersion to the maximum depth it must withstand.

(3) Depth of the water. It is always necessary to measure accurately the depth of the water at the point where the cache is to be placed. This will be the submersion depth if the cache is designed so that the container rests on the bottom of the lake or river. The container may be suspended some distance above the bottom, but the depth of the water must be known in order to determine the length of moorings connecting the container to the anchors.

(4) High- and low-water marks. Any tidal or seasonal changes in the depth of the water should be estimated as accurately as possible. It is especially important to consider the low-water mark, to insure that low water will not leave the cache exposed. The high-water point also should be considered to make sure that the increased depth will not crush the container or prevent recovery.

(5) Type of bottom. The bed of the lake or river in the vicinity of the cache should be probed as thoroughly as possible. If the bottom is soft and silty, the cache may sink into the muck, become covered with sediment, or drift out of place. If the bottom is rocky or covered with debris, the moorings may become snagged. Any of these conditions might make recovery very difficult.

(6) Water motion. Tides, currents, and waves should be considered, because any water motion will put additional strain on the moorings of the cache. It is important that the moorings be strong enough to withstand the greatest possible strain. If the water motion tends to rock the cache, special care must be taken to prevent the moorings from rubbing and fraying.

(7) Clearness of the water. How far the cache can be seen through the water must be considered in deciding how deeply to submerge it. If the water is quite clear, it may be necessary to camouflage the cache by painting the container to match the bottom. (Shiny metallic fixtures always should be painted a dull color.) Very murky water, on the other hand, will impede recovery by divers.

(8) Freezing of the water. Seasonal changes in the temperature of the water must be considered, because freezing might make recovery impossible in winter. The dates when the lake or river usually freezes and thaws should be determined as accurately as possible.

(9) Salt water. Since seawater is much more corrosive than fresh water, tidal estuaries and lagoons should not be used for caching. The only exception is the maritime resupply operation, where equipment may be submerged temporarily along the seacoast until it can be recovered by a shore party.

3-3. CONCEALMENT PROCEDURE

a. There are so many different ways of concealing objects in natural or ready-made hiding places that it is useless to generalize exact procedures for emplacement. For instance, if one were hiding weapons and ammunition in a cave, relying entirely on natural concealment, the emplacement operation would be reduced to simply locating the site. No tools would be needed except paper, pencil, and a flashlight. On the other hand, if one were sealing a packet of jewels in a brick wall, one would need a skilled mason, his kit of tools, and a supply of mortar expertly mixed to match the original.

b. Planning for concealment requires the greatest familiarity with local residents and their customs, and actual emplacement requires the utmost vigilance to detect observers. The final sterilization of the site is especially important, since a concealment site is usually open to frequent observation.

3-4. CACHING COMMUNICATIONS EQUIPMENT

a. General. As a general rule, the whole kit of equipment for a particular operational purpose (demolitions, survival, etc.) should be included in one container. Some equipment, however, is so sensitive from a security standpoint that the kit should be divided among two or more containers to minimize the danger that the whole kit will be discovered by the opposition. This is particularly true of communications equipment, since under some circumstances anyone who acquires a whole R/T set with the signal plan and cryptographic material would be able to play the set back. An especially dangerous type of penetration would be the result. In the face of this danger, the signal plan and the cryptographic material would never be placed in the same container, and ideally a communications kit should be distributed among three containers. If three containers are used, the distribution might be as follows:

(1) Container #1: The R/T set, including the crystals.

(2) Container #2: The signal plan and operational supplies for the R/T operator, such as currency, barter items, and small arms.

(3) Container #3: The cryptographic material.

b. Dispersion. When several containers are used for one set of equipment, they must be placed far enough apart so that if one is discovered, the others will not be detected in the immediate vicinity. On the other hand, they should be located close enough together so that they can be recovered conveniently in one operation. The distance between containers will depend on the particular situation, but ordinarily it should be at least ten meters. One final reference point ordinarily is used for a multiple cache. (See Sketch 5, illustrating the use of one round FRP and a compass azimuth to pinpoint a multiple cache, and sketch 13 showing how three corners on a rectangular FRP can pinpoint a multiple cache without using a compass azimuth.) One should be careful to avoid placing multiple caches in a repeated pattern. Discovery of one multiple cache would give the opposition a guide for probing others placed in a similar pattern.

3-5. THE CACHE REPORT

a. Purpose. The final, indispensable step in every emplacement operation is the preparation of a cache report that records the essential data for recovery. It is essential that the cache report provide all the information that someone unfamiliar with the locality would need to find his way to the site, recover the cache, and return safely.

b. Content. The most important parts of the cache report are the instructions for finding and recovering the cache. It should also include any other information that will facilitate planning the recovery operation. Since the details will depend upon the situation and the particular needs of each organization, the exact format of the report cannot be prescribed. The "Twelve-Point Cache Report" is intended merely to point out the minimum essential data. Whatever format is used, the importance of scrupulous attention to detail cannot be overemphasized. A careless error or omission in the cache report may make it impossible to recover the cache when it is needed.

c. Procedure. Since the recovery data is essentially the same as the information required for planning the emplacement operation, as much data as possible should be gathered during the personal reconnaissance for selecting the site. It is also advisable to draft the cache report before emplacement. This exercise will reveal the omissions. Then the missing data can be obtained during the visit to the site for emplacement. If this procedure is followed, the preparation of the final cache report will be reduced to an after-action check, to make sure that the cache actually was placed precisely where planned and that all other descriptive details are accurate. This ideal may seldom be realized, in actuality, but two procedures always should be followed:

(1) First, the final cache report should be completed as soon as possible after emplacement, so that all details will be fresh in mind.

(2) Second, the instructions for locating the cache should be checked promptly by someone who has not visited the site previously, in order to make sure that they are unmistakably clear. If someone participates in the emplacement operation who did not visit the site previously, he can check the instructions by using them to lead the party to the site. When no such person is available, it is advisable for someone to visit the site shortly after emplacement, provided he can do so securely. If the cache has been emplaced at night, a visit to the site in daylight may also provide an opportunity to check on the sterilization of the site.

CHAPTER 4

RECOVERY

4-1. GENERAL

Since the procedure for recovering a cache is generally similar to that for
emplacement, it need not be described in full. However, there are several
important considerations that should be stressed in training for a recovery
operation:

a. Practical Exercises. Anyone who is expected to serve as a recovery
agent should have the experience of actually recovering dummy caches, if field
exercises can be arranged securely. Complete mastery of the several
techniques for pinpointing a cache is especially desirable. This is best
attained by practice in selecting points of emplacement and in drafting as
well as following instructions.

b. Equipment. Although the equipment needed for recovery is generally
the same as that used in emplacement, it is important to consider what
additional items may be required and to include them in the cache report. A
probe rod may not be essential for emplacement, but it is definitely necessary
to carry to the site some object roughly the same size as the cache container,
for filling the cavity left in the ground by removal of a buried cache. Some
sort of container or wrapping material may be needed to conceal the recovered
material while it is being carried from the cache site to a safehouse.
Recovery of a submerged cache may require grappling lines and hooks,
especially if it is heavy.

c. Sketch of the Site. If possible, the recovery agent should be
provided with sketches of the cache site and the route to the site. If he
must rely exclusively on verbal instructions, as is the case when
communications are limited to R/T messages, he should draw a sketch of the
site before starting on the recovery operation. He should use all the data in
the verbal instructions to make the sketch as realistic as possible. Drawing
the sketch will help to clarify any misunderstanding of the instructions, and
when he goes to the site the sketch can be followed more easily than verbal
instructions. It may also be helpful for the recovery agent to draw a sketch
of the route from the IRP to the site, but he should not carry it on his
person because of the danger that it might direct the opposition to the cache,
if he were apprehended on the way.

d. Preliminary Reconnaissance. It may be advisable to check the
instructions for locating the cache, especially when the recovery operation
must be performed under stringent enemy controls or as quickly as possible,
with no extra time allowed for searching. Careful analysis of the best
available map can minimize reconnoitering activity in the vicinity of the
cache and thus reduce the danger of arousing suspicion. If recovery must be
done at night, the recovery agent should locate the cache by daylight and
place an unnoticeable marker directly over the cache.

e. Probing. Waste of critical time digging at the wrong spot can be avoided by using a probe rod before starting to dig. The probe rod should be pushed into the ground by hand, so that it will not puncture the container; the probe rod should never be pounded with a hammer. Pounding can be avoided by turning the probe rod while pushing it into the ground.

f. Digging and Refilling the Hole. The recovery procedure is the same as for burial, except for two points. First, a pick should never be used for digging the hole, since it might puncture the container and damage the cache material. Second, when refilling the hole after recovery, there is a problem of providing material to fill the cavity left by the container, rather than disposing of excess soil, as must be done after burial. Sometimes it is possible to fill the cavity with rocks, sticks, or other objects readily available at the site. If none are found during the preliminary reconnaissance and it is operationally necessary to leave no indication that a cache has been recovered, the recovery agent should carry to the site an object roughly the same size as the cache container.

g. Sterilizing the Site. As with emplacement, the whole recovery operation should be performed in such a way that no traces of the operation will be left at the site. Although sterilizing is not so vitally important for recovery as for emplacement, it should be done as thoroughly as time permits because evidence that a cache has been recovered might alert the opposition to covert activity in the area and provoke countermeasures.

APPENDIX A

TWELVE-POINT CACHE REPORT

1. Type of Cache—the component for which the cache is intended (guerrilla unit, sabotage cell, operator) and the functional purpose of the cached material (weapons, demolitions, communications).

2. Method of Caching—burial, concealment, or submersion.

3. Contents—an itemized list of all materials in each container, with a description of how each item is packaged.

4. Description of Containers—the size, weight, and other descriptive details. If several containers are included in the cache, each container should be assigned a number that appears on the sketch of the cache so that each container is identified by reference to its position in the cache.

5. General Area—the generally recognizable place names. Ordinarily they include the country, province, and smaller political divisions, down to the nearest town or village.

6. Immediate Area—the immediate reference point (IRP) and instructions for proceeding from the IRP to the final reference point (FRP). All landmarks that facilitate visual recognition of the route should be described.

7. Cache Location—the FRP and the exact sightings, linear measurements, etc., for pinpointing the cache. All measurements must be stated in the linear units (meters, feet) that the recovery agent can understand and use.

8. Emplacement Details—all features of the site or natural conditions that must be considered for physically retrieving the cache. The following represent the essentials, depending upon the method of caching:

   a. Burial—exact depth underground of each container; precise description of shoring (if used); all known seasonal variations (surface vegetation, date and depth of ground freezing and thawing). The type of soil and the time required for emplacement also provide useful guides for planning the recovery operation.

   b. Concealment—exactly how the cache is placed in the site and any physical covering (plaster, bricks) that must be penetrated or removed to recover the cache. Full instructions should be provided if removing or replacing the covering involves any special problems or techniques (matching the plaster or mortar). All necessary information about a custodian, if one is used, should be included.

   c. Submersion—depth of the water (including high- and low-water marks); submersion depth (if the container does not rest on the bottom of the lake or river); type of bottom; water motion; clearness of the water; usual freezing and thawing dates.

9. Operational Data and Remarks--list of equipment needed for recovery of the cache; description of at least two routes to the site that offer maximum natural concealment and means of escape in case of sudden attack; nearby houses and thoroughfares; description of local security forces, their regular posts and patrol routes in the vicinity of the cache; suggestions for action cover when visiting the site, including warning of what cover to avoid; any other information that may facilitate planning the recovery operation. Special consideration should be given to any equipment that may be needed for recovery, even though it was not used in emplacement.

10. Dates of Emplacement and Duration of the Cache--based on an estimate of how long the contents of the cache will remain usable. Pertinent factors include: the normal shelf life of items that deteriorate with time (medicine, batteries); the expiration date of official documents (passports, licenses); how long the packaging will withstand moisture penetration, corrosion, etc.

11. Sketches and Diagrams--whatever sketches and diagrams are necessary to illustrate the instructions for locating the cache and the description of the cache. These should include at least an area sketch, showing the route from the IRP to the FRP (see Sketch 12), and a site diagram, showing precisely how the cache is pinpointed (see Sketch 13). Photographs of the immediate area, the IRP, FRP, and other landmarks in the vicinity of the site are not essential, but they may be quite helpful.

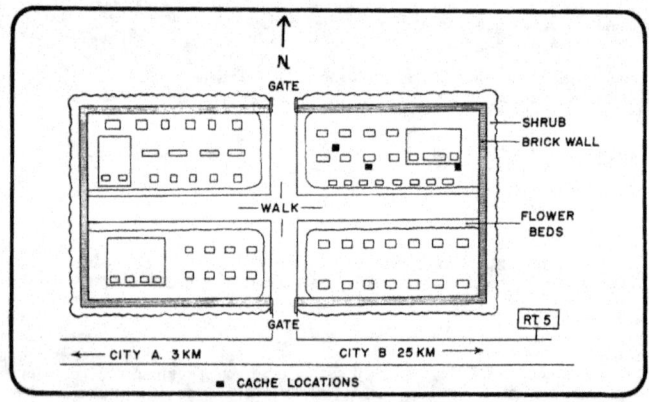

Sketch 12. Cache locations.

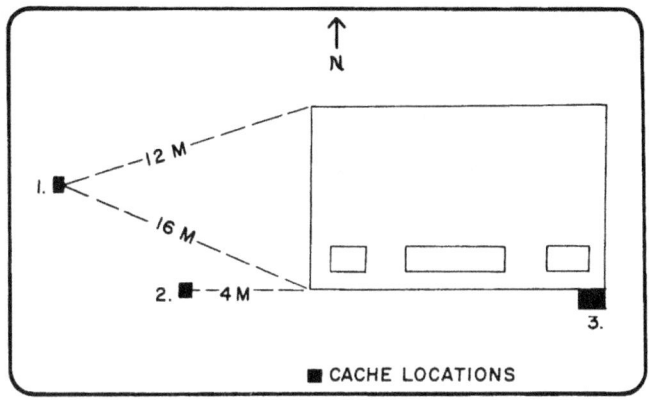

CACHE LOCATIONS

Sketch 13. Cache locations.

12. Radio Message for Recovery—useful to have such a message drafted in case an emergency dictates its use, even though a radio message may never be required for recovery. The best time for drafting the message is when the details are fresh in the mind of the emplacer. The radio message should include: type of cache, method of caching, and concise instructions for locating the site. The acid test of these instructions is whether they can be reduced to a message that is unmistakably clear, but brief enough for secure radio transmission. Very careful consideration must be given to the intended recovery agent's familiarity with the area as well as what maps and makeshift surveying instruments will be available to him. The message must be in a language he is sure to understand; it must be drafted or translated by someone who is fluent in the language. The following radio message gives instructions for recovering the three-point cache illustrated in sketches 12 and 13.

> COMMO CACHE IN THREE HOLES IN "Y" PROVINCE "X"
> COUNTRY IN CEMETERY THREE KILOMETERS EAST CITY
> "A" ON NORTH SIDE ROUTE FIVE. CACHE IS IN
> NORTHEAST CORNER NEAR WALLED PLOT. CONTAINER
> ONE IS WEST OF PLOT ONE TWO METERS FROM
> NORTHWEST CORNER AND ONE SIX METERS FROM
> SOUTHWEST CORNER. CONTAINER TWO IS FOUR METERS
> WEST OF SOUTHWEST CORNER IN LINE WITH SOUTH
> SIDE. CONTAINER THREE IS ON SOUTH SIDE
> ADJACENT TO SOUTHEAST CORNER OF PLOT.

This sample message is intended to illustrate the absolute minimum of data that ordinarily is essential for recovery. Additional data should be included in a radio message only when special circumstances require it. For instance, if a cached package is too heavy or too large for one man to carry, the weight or the exterior dimensions should be included. The depth of a submerged cache ordinarily should be specified, but the depth of a buried cache should not be included unless it is buried deeper than the usual 45 centimeters.

NOTE: The Need for Professional Competence--ultimate success of the caching operation may well depend upon attention to details that may seem of minor importance to the nonprofessional eye. Security factors such as the cover of the caching party, the sterility of the material cached, and the obliteration of even the slightest trace of the operation are vital. Highly important, too, are the technical factors that govern the preservation of the material in usable condition and the recording of data essential for recovery. Successful caching entails scrupulous adherence to the basic principles of clandestine operations as well as familiarity with the technicalities of the operation. These high standards of security and "know-how" must be instilled through meticulous training.

048792-Brn

Notes

Notes

Notes

<u>**Notes**</u>

www.ingramcontent.com/pod-product-compliance
Lightning Source LLC
Chambersburg PA
CBHW060341290526
45793CB00003B/685